The Long Road to Nowhere

o.b.
thompson

.

The Long Road to Nowhere

2012-2020 Poetry Collection

O.B. Thompson

ISBN: 978-0-6452161-1-0
Image © Samantha Graham
Published by WarmBreeze Digital Publishing.

Contents

Battles 99

Introspections   **139**

Foreword

I don't believe that having a foreword in a book is all that important, I don't think I've ever read one. Yet, not having one also doesn't seem appropriate - so here we are. From what I do know of the craft, I believe that it is customary to discuss the concept of the book and why it is important to the author, so I guess that I'll start there.

The idea for this collection started some time ago during the period when I began to fall out of love with writing poetry. I honestly thought that I would never start writing again and that having a collection like this would be for the best to just amalgamate my work into one place for reasons of vanity. It could be considered that is still what I'm doing but as I forge ahead, I see this collection taking on more of a significant purpose than that. Not necessarily to anyone other than me, but more significant nonetheless.

A favourite quotation of mine is from Cyril Conolly saying that it is "better to write for yourself and have no public, than to write for the public and have no self." As something of a completely unknown writer and someone who only ever really self-publishes their work, I must take heart from that. To even have any public at all is something that I do not take for granted and it is why I am always keen to share more and more of my work.

Going back and compiling this work has seen me take something of a stroll down memory lane, and while it hasn't always been pleasant - it has been enjoyable to reminisce and remind myself of memories long forgotten. Each chapter of this collection comprises of poetry from very distinct periods in my life - multiple rounds of heartache, internal struggles and a joyous appreciation of the world around me.

I can't say with any certainty that I love every single one of these poems or that each one is better than the last but they each tell a tale and I couldn't bring myself to cut any of them out. There have been edits, adjustments and changes - but none that significantly alter their meaning, at least not in any meaningful way.

Someone recently told me that kindness costs nothing and that I should be kinder to myself and for the first time in a long time, I am proud of myself and proud of this body of work. Although this is the majority of my life's literary work to date concealed within these pages, this is by no means the end. In fact, I hope it is only the beginning.

Wherever, whenever or however you're reading this, thank you. It means a lot to me that you have taken the time to read some of this collection of poetry.

For all those friends and family members who travelled alongside me on the long road to nowhere.

The End of Beginnings

Costly

Diamonds in her eyes,
Flowers in her hands,
I saw it end right then and there.

Tears of value roll down her blissful cheek,
Her heart of gold shatters.

Br*eaks.*
Falls.
Destroyed.

Never mind girl, there's always tomorrow.

Burn Me

O mighty temptress challenge me,
Upon thy hearty flame;
I've said it once that only it can be;
You that bares that task to tame
The ghost of you and me.

Extinguish me with thy breath,
I am a wounded flame;
Oh my faded heart shines but once;
Anxiously glowingly in the tenderness of your beauty.

I found nothing of myself in you;
But everything of you in me.

The Sound of Music

From angels lips comes her heavenly call;
Impossible to resist;
It glides in the night,
And settles softly on my humbled ear.
Whisks me off my listless feet,
And forward to her arms.

A thousand tiny harps,
Play ballads in my captivated heart.
Her resonance strikes fear,
In the hearts of misunderstanding men
But caresses the souls of those tragic few held dear.

A wave carries me to sea,
As her forgiving voice washes over me.

Purple Haze

My purple vision haunts the lonely nights;
Stirring quietly,
Moving briskly,
A wondrous lust takes hold.

Butterflies begin to rise,
She stalks the night of which she hunts.

A perfect vision of a beautiful trap,
She takes me quietly within her jaws,
The silent night is no more.

Enticed.
Entrapped.

I am servant nor master
We are one in the same
Take this night slow, my love,
It may never come again.

Shining Example

The night shines on her
Soft, elegant beauty;
Moves freely in the night;
Eyes aglow;
Heart beating to a different rhythm.

Battle cries echo on secretive fortress walls;
Hands grip tightly to love's salvation;
Piercing eyes tell their own tale;

No more anger, betrayal or fear;
Chin up, my love
It only gets better from here.

A solitary kiss
Spills a thousand words into yearning ears,
And hungry mouths swallow them whole.

Love is not a matter of the body but of the mind;
It can be cruel, painful,
But sometimes kind.

Unwittingly it could take years to find,
And sometimes you will be wise;
To look right before your disbelieving eyes.

Mountain Lion

Hear the call of the ravenous mountain lions,
On the famous hills,
I come from far and wide to make my devotion;
To the pillars of my satisfaction.

Contemplative views fill me with pleasure,
The succulent taste of fresh crisp air soothes my aching
lungs,
A mountain lion roars,
I climb the hill again.

In the Fire

In the fire,
We burn together;
Bodies entwined,
In a passion of blazing heat.

Burning long into the night,
Flames roar;
It grows louder,
And the fire burns wildly,
Uncontrollably;
We burn together.

Older and Wiser

Older and wiser,
Love doesn't bless me,
It haunts me.

It stalks me at every turn,
Appearing when I least expect it;
Just as I begin to settle without it;
Just as I think it's gone;
It rears its foul head to haunt me once more;
The ugly devil himself;
I know he laughs when I cry.

What have you ever done for me?
Why do we all seek to find you?
What has love ever done for us?

Yet,
I greet him like an old friend;
I serenade him like a lover;
Who would've thought it?

The ghastly ghoul of love;
He is my lover.

What has love ever done for me?
It brought me my only true love.

Rise & Fall

Beauty weaved on intangible threads;
Wilting golden where she treads;
She made sure my passion stirred;
The most beautiful song you've ever heard;
Surely it cannot be;
That this beautiful song is being sung to me?

My ears ached for the music;
My heart ached for the beauty;
If music is the food of love,
Then my gut shall stay content;
For all the world can but say;
For certain love I never meant.

Happy, healthy, hearty music feeds my heart once more;
My soul is nourished not by the beauty I cannot see,
But the one who once stood in front of me.

Phoenix rise, phoenix die;
This love shall burn forever.
No time shall come when one can't hear,
Our silent golden melody.

Now I see how I was blind;
And given time I found something worth calling mine;
It goes to show,
Life can be kind, sometimes.

Pearl

Flowing locks on grand shoulders;
There are none more beautiful,
Nor bolder.
Tender neck of aches and pains;
Caressed with care;
Make a man feel home again.

A smile shy with eyes so wide;
You catch them staring,
With nowhere to hide.
A single spot of happiness,
Upon a lonely face;
Does nothing but impress.

A heavenly scent;
A charm so wild;
You must be from the angels sent.

Whoever stands by you,
Hand in hand,
Will be the only lucky man.

Look in the mirror,
Smile and say,
We're going to change the world some day.

Forlorn

A beauty of humbled divinity,
Controls the destiny,
Of the weakest man she ever met.

He sits and waits,
For a silent call,
It falls on deaf ears.
Whispered on castrated tongues.
Lonely he sits;
By the window once more,
Longing for the beauty,
Which he does so adore.

Extroverted Expectations

In public we exist
As a mockery of ourselves
And seek only to cater to those
Who will laugh with us.
In private we exist
In our true form;
Alone
And desperate for laughter.

Crawl

I'd kill myself a thousand times,
To give you life;
Without you there is no I.

I want to crawl inside you and die;
Where I thought I had everything;
I now have nothing.

Never Again

The warm touch of the perfect embrace,
Is long gone now;
A distant memory.
My hope has thinned,
And realisations of loneliness set in.

My heart is bleak,
My fight is weak,
I've lost the will to win.

Oeillet Noir

Some things are hard to forget,
The glint of the sun
On despairing eyes,
Is definitely one.

A false smile,
Betrayed by your demeanour,
As you sit,

Silent

Staring through me,
I'm reminded that,
Sometimes quiet is violent,
And everything must end in time.

Confusion

Why am I scared to speak up for my feelings?

Living in contempt of my heart,
Every day is harder than the last.

A tongue tied in sorrow,
Scrambled thoughts boundless.
Things may be better soon;
Just not tomorrow.

3 Weeks Happy

As the past dawned;
You answered its call.
I found myself sinking further,
Into someone I'm not;
And who you didn't want me to be.
When at first I felt free;
Now I only feel lost.

Wooden Heart

The splinters of a callous wooden heart,
Nestle deep inside,
A gaping, open wound.

Vulnerable.
Alone.

A cruel blow masterfully executed;
Fragility exposed, exploited.

An untrustworthy gaze,
Grows ever more sceptical.

With ominous delight,
She's out of sight,
And that cold wooden heart,
That tore me apart,
Will only strike again.

D.N.R

As I burned away,
The only sounds I heard,
Were all the things,
I swore I'd never say.

My heart is still,
Your morphine words,
Linger in the air before,
They make their final kill.

Devil on my Back

Plagues of devils come forth,
From behind locked doors,
Shrouded in mystery,
Covered in shame,
Unwilling to bend and play a fair game.

Shot down in anger,
With aggrieved nostrils flared,
Speaking false gospel,
On how angels never cared.

Their fall from grace mighty,
Now they're drowning in lust,
And while they struggle for breath,
The angel stands laughing,
As they sink to their death.

Regret?

With sincerity,
I hope I was no mistake,
Like you said he was.

Warning

Give yourself to others;
Don't let them take you.
We are our own,
To have and to hold.
At the end of the day,
Who will love you at the end,
That girl who always went away?
For my heart just cannot mend,
What you took from me.

Give yourself to others;
Don't let them take you.
If we hold our own,
There's nothing they can do.
Who will love you at the end
The one who stuck it through?
Do not give yourself to others,
Only you can always be there for you.

Foghorns

I missed the foghorns on the river this morning,
It's been quite warm recently,
So it came as a surprise to me that I missed them.

I hate the way they wake me,
I hate the way they sound,
I hate the way they seem to hate me.

I hated them then,
I hate them now,
Yet nothing I have found,
Can replace their unique sound.

They rouse me from my bed,
I stare out of the window,
And listen out to no avail;
Where is my favourite sound?

I must point out I'm not insane,
Just lovesick once again.

Who'd have thought I could miss something that I hate so
much?

The Note

If I died now,
How much time would I save?

Secrets haunting my mind,
I'll take them to an early grave.
Slipping further to a maddening darkness,
Never to be clean again,
With everything to lose,
And nothing to gain.

Nothing left to do,
In a life that is nothing without you.

One Too Many Times

A mirage of false
dissatisfaction filters through
the eyes of mutually disenchanted lovers;
obliged to divulge
incorrect assumptions
of shared disinterest;
in a thinly veiled attempt
to mask contempt.

I'm done.

A Souvenir

Tender magnificence,
Holds the key to a thousand smiles.

Hands shake,
Bodies ache,
For the simple caress.

Poetry in motion,
Does no justice to perfect form,
Just as disbelievers do no justice to themselves.

Behold the beauty ten thousand sonnets cannot explain;
This is no sonnet my dear,
Just a love letter; a souvenir.

Of everything we have;
Of everything we had;
Of everything I lost.

In Contradiction

I am no longer scared of love,
A life without love,
Is a life not loved at all.
I was dying to live,
Love set me free,
The façade crumbled,
Under the haze of glory days,
Set my weary love ablaze,
Fear gone without a trace,
I found meaning in a world I had no place.

It gave me a fright,
When our love first took flight,
But now I feel just like a bird.
Did I just write that?
Man,
How absurd.

Identity Card

On that old marble floor;
I found a key,
Used no more.
The key to my heart
Is rusted and forgotten;
As it was from the start.

Last time that I gave it away,
It ended up here;
On that old marble floor;
From now on I'll keep it near.

Learn from my mistake;
Hold yourself in high regard;
Keep your heart to yourself;
Your very own identity card.

Swansong

For one last time,
The pen runs dry,
Nothing left to say,
Will change the mind,
Of you or I.

A solemn end,
To macabre bliss,
Tired minds are dazed,
In the chaos,
Of all of this.

Love forcibly imposed,
Can never run as deep,
As the memories,
Of burned out loves,
That you insist you must keep.

Your rosy cheeks,
Grace this disheartened page,
For one last time,
Not in anger,
Nor in rage.

This might be a swansong;
But please don't sing along.

Twenty Four

6:14 a.m.

Awake before the dawn again,
But did I even fall asleep?

These nights begin to blur together;
My vision thins;
My brow furrows;
Why is this happening to me?

There are infinite thoughts alive;
But knowing I'm not good enough;
Triumphs in the stakes
To ruin my morning.

One day you might return to me;
But I do not hold my breath;
For madness that way lies.

The dawn breaks;
And so do I.

Why is this happening to me?

07:34 a.m.

Woke up with a smile upon my face,
For the first time in a while.
The heat's died down upon us,
With nobody staring,
Criticizing every move we make,
And yet I still can't seem to beat this sinking feeling.

10:21 a.m.

I couldn't sleep last night;
For thoughts of you.
Everything I planned to say;
If only you knew.

I don't know why I do it to myself;
But somehow I do.
Maybe I'm waiting in vain;
For you to want me too.

12:23 p.m.

As my mind drifts to you,
And back again,
Your words ring loudly in my ears
Yet hollow all the same.
My love can only grow,
A love that I do not want to tame.

3:13 p.m.

Everyone in my life exudes stability;
Which is reflected in my overwhelming ability;
To attract fragility;
And really what I want right now;
Is not to aggravate the hostility
Between myself and my internal futility.

Which in turn decides my fate;
But now I cannot wait to return home;
To a state where I can renegotiate;
The possibility that everything;
I've been feeling of late;
Has been a result of what I know.
Now to be a distinct inability;
Just to let go.

The Six O'Clock News

Once I had a halo but then it caught on fire.
Once I met a leader but then he committed genocide.
Once I met a deaf man but he was disgraced to hear that the
world had turned to shit.

8:37 p.m.

When the sun goes down,
This lonely heart alights.
For this heavenly darkness is aglow,
With the wings of an angel,
Whom stills a beating heart with eyes of splendour.

A loving tongue speaks gentle words,
Her beauty trumps all doubt,
And love pours out.

Is it a dream?
Long may it continue.

For life without this angel is nothing but a nightmare;
So please don't wake me up.

9:58 p.m.

I turned to Satan because God wouldn't listen any more;
But in the end he shut me out;
I guess that eventually we all get tired;
Of hearing people talking about;
Problems that no one wants to hear.

Let me get this straight,
I never loved God or Satan,
I just needed company.

Who can honestly say they never needed company?

10:16 p.m.

It took me all day,
To write one fucking haiku,
Now I cannot stop.

11:07 p.m.

My mind is blank,
From over thinking.
  I thought I could see clearly,
  But my vision is still blurred,
  You know I loved you dearly.

11:31 p.m.

Some nights;
I go to bed happy.
Some nights;
I go to bed sad.

But every night,
I go to bed glad,
That I could ever share it with you.

12:53 a.m.

I still get sad,
From time to time.

You'll never know,
How bad I feel,
Knowing all the bullshit mistakes;
Were nobody's fault
But mine.

1:07 a.m.

The fall is further than the drop,
I'm clinging on for dear life,
Not that my life's worth much.

Might as well just let go then.

1:32 a.m.

Here I sit by the window,
On this cold lonely night,
With my hand down my pants;
Looking out below at
All the people scurrying like ants.

3:05 a.m.

Fighting with sleep,
Never brought me much peace.
Should I try counting sheep?
Or maybe count geese?

What's the point?

I can't sleep.

The Great Divide

My New Love

My new love is much the same;
And though I know not her name;
I know I've felt like this before;
It could be once, twice or maybe more.

Her gentle touch rests on fractured skin,
And brings upon a familiar skin;
Because deep down I know,
She will follow me wherever I go.

My new love is much the same;
I've got that feeling once again;
She's here to save me from uncertain fate;
I only pray she's not too late.

Amethyst

A glamorous ray of light,
Shines through dark clouds,
And warms the land below.

It glistens on the horizon,
With an air of unknowing beauty.

Such attainment
Lies beyond the grasp;
Of every humble passer by.

Lightning cracks,
And thunder rolls.

The clouds disguise the light,
As something not quite right.

Dreaming

A dream too perfect,
Is never positive.
Unreachable glories hold no significance
In the cold light of day.

Tempting, maybe;
But ultimately too far.

Reach out and touch the air,
These dreams are never fair,

Riding to New York

As I rode to New York;
A single streetlight
Lit the way in the fog.

It flickered in the cool autumn wind,
Dimming further in the aching grey,
A shimmering mirage,
Too feeble to touch,
Not bright enough to see,
All that I could tell;
Was that it was calling out to me.

The Work of an Angel

Delightful sounds on pricked ears,
Echo through eternity.
Housed walls speak in tongues,
With the grace of an angel.

The music hits the feet of the sullen,
Who dance once again
Like men possessed
With joy not anger.

Feet alight on top of the world;
Nothing can bring them down.

A World Away

Eyes to light a thousand lanterns,
Carved onto a canvas,
Of picture perfect delight.

A smile only smiled once,
Reveals haunted lilies rest on silken cheek,
Her china soul drifts ever further,
Across the bloated sea.

Standing oceanside,
Loud calls get no reply,
Two lovers separated by the malevolent tide;
Brought together by unfathomable waves;
Of tribal passion
Ingrained in every fibre.

Although they rarely share a day,
Two lovers still celebrate each other,
From half a world away.

Whispers

A whisper of love,
Turns the mind three times forward,
And three times back.

Nothing can be sure,
But looking into the mirror,
And seeing the reflection of two;
Is more than enough to know.

Voices

When I speak to myself,
I only say one thing.
When the voices in my head speak,
They only say one thing.

Calling out to you,
Like a whisper in the wind;
Call me crazy;
But the sound is getting louder.

O Life, the Mistress

Life seems cruel,
In the face of unimaginable defeat;
But even the greatest of disappointments,
Can have a significantly positive impact,
On the person we want to be,
Overcoming the person who suffered in defeat.

The Great Divide

Though every day,
A haunted ship takes flight,
We try with all our might,
To shrink this great divide
Of oceans long,
And oceans wide.

Pictures speak a thousand words;
But when only three words spoken,
Will truly please;
What good is a picture sent across the seas?

Though the senses flare,
It is no substitute for touch,
There is only one thing left to do,
And I would drink the entire ocean;
To be again with you.

Bed of Roses

Gentle goddess,
Cheeks carved in stone,
Blushed with rose,
Fragranced with Myrrh;
Make earthly scholars blush
In days first light.

As the silent sun stirs;
And peaks to end a lovers rest;
Even in fresh dawn,
She lies in quiet beauty;
Unbeknownst to what grace,
Belies her perfect cheek.

Much Travelled

A brilliant candle,
Flickers boldly in the distance,
Nothing more than a mirage;
Yet its warmth fills a lonely heart;
More attainable than anything,
That a young man could ever have.

Winds flicker the fierce flames;
And a storm brews in the distance;
A lonely traveller must rest his head;
With nothing but candlelight,
To guide the much trodden path.

Twinkle

Kind eyes that have seen so much;
Twinkle under shared moonlight;
Glistening from afar.

Their enticing glance,
Seems too good to be true,
But still they call my name.
I'm wary of those tired eyes,
Yet excited all the same.

Sunday Mornings

Entwined in perfect solitude;
Crisp golden sheets,
Encase two precisely pieced bodies,
Exploring their souls together,
On this perfect Sunday morning.

Sun warms the toes,
Sparks between lips warm the heart;
The smell of black coffee drifts in;
But nobody will leave their bed,
On this perfect Sunday morning.

Lazy lovers lie together,
On this perfect Sunday morning.

Sewn Fields

Buckets drain the empty waterfall;
Rain falls on sullen ground;
No crops will spring here,
The season's over now I fear.

Valiant seeds drift on the wind;
Their weary legs carry no more;
With heavy eyes and fallen smiles,
They rest where they can see for miles.

Venus

As I ventured to the river lands;
I found myself infatuated,
Butterflies filled an empty head,
And spines tingled,
With the queen's gentle touch.

The river flowed toward me;
And as I struggled to breathe;
I saw the light;
She smiled down;
And I began to drown,
In the pools of Venus' eyes;
I felt safe for one last time;
I knew that she was mine.

Yhi

As the light dies,
So too the flower,
Hear its cries.

Out of withering darkness
And shrunken hearts,
Leaps forth an excess of a light,
To reignite a long diminished fire;
Laid to ash by cruelty;
Restored by beauty;
Now the flames burn long and bright;
In glorious day;
And transcendent night.

Now the flowers grow again,
To see their beauty,
Keeps humbled men sane.

Night Owl

The haunting nature of golden darkness;
Speaks volumes in the eerie quiet;
Contemplative evenings,
Become indecisive breakfasts;
With plenty of food for thought.

And a night of indignation,
Becomes a morning of self-pity.
Every thought like this could mean something;
Or it could mean nothing at all.

The Follower

Without shared light,
Our paths rarely cross,
But the beauty of your thought,
Brings radiance to the night.

An intolerable silence rings hollow,
So we fill it with deafening memories,
There is no place on earth,
Where each other we would not follow.

When heaven and hell collide,
And the earth doth shake,
I will hold you close,
To keep you by my side.

LMc

Unrecognisable cohesion
Reigns supreme;
Amongst two distant souls
Bonded by passion;
Across hellish water;
Outside the predictable
Bonds of every new dawn.

Sands

As seconds tick away,
Millennia pass slowly before waiting eyes,
Fixed on the fading hands,
Of the withering clock,
Haunted by an everlasting sound.

Tick, tock
Tick, tock

The sands of time run slower now,
As though they've taken solemn vow,
To persecute the dreamer.

First and Only

Not so subtle passion burns bright;
All throughout the night.

An eternal existence;
Regardless of the distance.

So remember one thing;
To our memories you'll cling.

But when you're feeling sad and lonely;
Remember you're my first and only.

The Quest

When water floods a lovers dream,
Shattered fortunes no longer what they seemed.
He mounts a quest,
His heart possessed.

With an angel down below
And with his puzzled heart in tow;
He searches high and low;
Across the sea;
For what they said could never be;
Yet he travelled all the while,
To see a goddess smile.

Summer

As the summer rolled into view;
I felt my heart skip three beats
At the sight of you.

Long flowing hair,
Laying gently on your shoulder;
My lungs ran out of air.

With eyes to melt the sun;
And when they first lay on me
I knew you were the one.

For us we will stay strong;
And be there every day,
Just to prove ourselves wrong.

Pine

Pine scent rolls in,
On a gentle breeze,
Through the slightly cracked window,
To cleanse a sticky summer sun.

It dances on the senses;
And leaves a happy mark.

The cool air of night,
Fills me with warmth,
As I begin my evening dance with darkness.

Dance With Angels

The beauty of your soul
Lights the dim path
Through the troubled times,
Burning into open wounds,
And seeping into a cracked heart.

Words of comfort,
Hold me close,
As I live in new delight,
Reveling in the angelic glory,
Shining from eyes so bright.

Laugh with me;
Live with me;
Let me hold you quietly.

Clock Tales

The mind ticks over slowly,
In the silence of the lonely night,
Thoughts turn to you.

Visions of glorious being;
Dance passionately on the brain.

Toying and teasing,
Through the glimmer of the faded light,
I want to crawl inside my head;
And hold you tight.

Angel Delight

My angel is alive,
Forever dangling on the tip of my tongue;
Running through the forest,
Of everlasting dreams.

Shimmering in the glistening sun;
Angel eyes,
Reflecting diamonds in their glory.

Diving to the deepest depth;
Of her perfection,
I fell into diamond covered love.

I Caught Fire

Invisible souls,
Fail to keep implausible promises;
And hang me out to dry,
In the gentle breeze,
That serves little but to fan the flames,
Of discontent that have taken over,
And engulfed me.

A mind on fire is inconsolable;
And nonsensical.

Calligraphy on Crinkled Paper

The pen dances,
For its perfect mistress,
And paints in tongues,
What words could never satisfy,
To illuminate perfection;
Wherever she may be.

For All The World

I long for dreams of you;
A glistening beam,
In moments of darkest blue;
Everything gets better or so it may seem.

It may be that my happiness relies;
On everything I see,
When I stare into those radiant eyes;
But as the world stares back at me,
Behind its perfect frame;
All I really need to know,
Is that nothing will ever be the same.

Divinity

Heart of gold, beauty divine;
A glimmer of hope to those who shine;
Not as quite as bright as you;
Who cry alone when days are through.

Paper skin entrenches bones of steel;
That shows us how to shake off and deal;
With earthly horrors unbound;
And yet my eyes your strength does confound.

That steel below inside so firm,
Shakes my heart to now affirm,

You are the woman in the dream;
That sadly it begins to seem;
Will likely stay, only a dream.

Behind Sad Eyes

Oh, sad eyes;
Dry your tears not mine.

A fluorescent beauty,
Harbours a gracious soul,
Encumbered by sadness,
Endowed with love.

Everyone is sad sometimes;
But nothing lasts forever;
You're only human darling;
We'll fight this world together.

Never smiling,
Never sad,
To be endowed with your wisdom,
Makes men only glad,
That they've never seen you smile,
Through swollen eyes;
Flood rivers of love,
Reaching far and wide.

Angel of my Nightmare

Here comes the wicked night again,
Snapping at my heels,
A blinding darkness startles.

Every now and then
Tired eyes begin to tremble;
And cower in such fear,
Of the ever growing night,
That's really nothing special.

Although my eyes are scared to close;
I know I'll dream of
Hair of brown
And cheeks of rose.
In that moment there,
I know I'm safe;
For watching over me;
Is the angel of my nightmare.

White Russian

An angel in the mist,
Enchanting beauty,
Moving slowly in her haunting manner.
Hold her tight;
Before she flees again;
Into the darkness of this sombre night.

Enticing all who cross her,
A mysterious smile that holds a thousand answers,
To questions unfathomable;
And never to be understood;
Back away slowly,
You've done all you could.

Picking Flowers

Sweet scented heaven,
Dances on the senses,
Trembling lips,
Desperate for a taste,
Of any sort of beauty;
That dares to shoot a fleeting glance.

Starved of sunlight,
And begging for attention,
A wilted rosebud rears his head,
"Nourish me, nourish me!"

He calls in hope,
But the moment's gone,
He fades away,
Until the sun comes around again.

Not Quite A Swan Song

The silent seconds ache;
And with heavenly words I wake;

In angelic form she lies;
Speaking from behind worldly eyes;

In comfort's arms I lay;
Going nowhere, here to stay;

Will you ever hang me out to dry?
My love, even if I could I would not even try.

Hold her with open arms;
Safe from all and any ghastly harms;

Speak quickly now my cherished one;
The songs of birds have just begun.

Observations

Declaration

I declare war on the world.

The entire human race,
The ones I've come to hate;
Who I'll stop at nothing to annihilate.

Time is going backwards;
I'm the only one who's thinking forwards;
It's nature versus nurture;
And we all know existence is torture;
So let's start the slaughter.

This world holds nothing as far as I can see;
Everyone walks around like the world owes them everything
for free,
But you are nothing you see,
I've made you everything you can and will be.

So how can it be that existence ends with me?

Soul in a Jar

So, the president's black.
And, that's nice, I guess.
But, haven't they all been black?

For I see not race;
But suits and souls.

Both of which boast expensive price tags;
Both are easily bought, easily sold;
Both are black, empty and cold;

I wouldn't get too excited just yet.

Dictionary

Words have no meaning to anyone but those who speak them.
Everyone thinks that their own words have greater meaning,
because without that we would have no art. But as I sit here
listening to an endless stream of clichés, I wonder if words
have any meaning at all. I mean; how can someone speak so
much but say so little?

Indictment

Selfie loving teens breeding uneducated fiends;
A generation of failure;
Breeds another generation governed by disgusting behaviour;
Kids out with more guns than an arsenal;
Our streets have turned farcical.
Here we are waiting,
For a legally clean cardinal,
To return order to the anarchical.

Fill a head with knowledge; not a bullet;
And acknowledge that there is a way out.

Life isn't a movie,
Life is a duty,
A cross we all must bear,
So why not make it fair?

Modern life is fucked;
And there's nothing I can do.

Modern life is fucked;
I could help but I really don't want to.

Terror on the Shores

I've got a feeling I've been lied to by the media,
And that video games and music;
Are not the cause of my hysteria.

I'm a product of my environment;
Nothing more, nothing less;
Than a servant to this tyrant;
That I see destroying the press.
The ones who try to oppress,
Those who refuse to tow the line.

While they tell us everything's fine;
Like a sadistic nursery rhyme;
They think the worlds gone blind,
But we're more awake than ever.

Your reign of terror can't last forever.

Title Censored

My life is in a state of perpetual motion,
A deadly cocktail of too much ineffectual emotion.

Even though these words I write they may seem intellectual;
One day they will be banned,
I know that is inevitable,
And my friend; that is regrettable.

Opulence

We live in the age of reason,
Yet knowledge swallows us whole,
We're collapsing under the force of the black tide,
Commercial arrogance is leprosy eating us alive.

We bow to the banker;
And we jail the thinker;
The end of days is nigh.

We will end in fire,
A selfish flame flickers,
We will end in their opulence.

Slaves to the rich;
Impoverished, alone
Scared.

Fear and Loathing

We speak in fear;
What good is a world where even the journalists cower?

It's the fault of the ninety nine per cent;
For not standing up and speaking without consent;
There's no need to reinvent the past or the present.

Only to speak the truth,
And turn general ignorance to general sentience,
So that I can finish my sentence without a gasp or a shriek.
"Can he say that?"
"Of course he can, let the man speak!"

Fly Away

Disenchanted constituents from broken homes,
Run rampant in the streets creating mindless violence,
As a method of disassembling government sponsored silence.

The eagle rules with an iron fist;
His rubber bullets are toys;
Presents for who try to resist;
He laughs at everything he destroys.

The uncensored populace,
Fly south for the winter,
And spread your wings,
Free speech is now a splinter;
Under the thumb of false kings.

Freedom fighters on an unseen battlefield,
Hunting the eagle for all he's concealed,
And all that's now illegal.

When he's caught,
His neck will snap,
Like a promise of prosperity,
And it will end this senseless scrap.

Flap,
Flap.

Snap,
Snap.

Identity Fraud

Where is our democracy? It's gone, replaced.
By a financial meritocracy;
And the profligacy of this downright hypocrisy,
Is burning my eyes like a girl who just opened the front door.
The world I knew isn't here anymore;
Whether you are rich or poor.

I feel so fucking distraught;
That there can be so much food for thought,
While there's people starving,
In countries whose bank balance reads below nought.
Because of the land we've raped and pillaged;
For oil we should have just bought.

Yet they take and they take;
When there's people struggling here in the land you hold
dear;
And for what? A cheaper pair of shoes?

This is what happens when the government choose to kill,
In the name of a God who's gone and left,
Because he was appalled at what you'd done in his name,
Now my life has become some type of identity fraud.

And I want my fucking money back.

Torches and Pitchforks

You lied one too many times,
The mob is on its way,
Torches and pitchforks at the ready;
Can something be your fault,
If you're only partly to blame?

They'll take you dead or alive,
You'll be famous,
For your heinous crimes against your own country,
Seek asylum south;
Because here you won't survive.

On Nature

Man by nature is timid,
Afraid of what he does not understand,
What he cannot understand,
What he cannot understand about himself.

Women by nature are not timid,
A woman's heart more accepting,
More human somehow,
She frightens man with power;
Oh, how they cower.

> I stand aside and laugh
> At the crying misogynist.

System Failure

How can you oppress the way that a woman wants to dress?
Because of a sick freak who says she deserved it?

When I hear words like that,
Our future seems bleak,
How can you have such cheek?
To spout crap like that,
It doesn't make you look innocent,
It makes you look weak.

Everything Goes Black

Sometimes the only thing you can do is laugh in the face of
something that is utterly devastating. On this occasion a knife
to the gut would have been more polite. I gambled everything
on you, and lost.

Recep

The self-important man makes the greatest fool,
For he has no failings,
And the mirror never lies,
He is blind from staring into the sun.

The self-important man can never be trusted,
A trivial life glorified by fear,
Some things are not as they appear,
Robbed blind by impotence,
Logic and reason gives way to narcissistic importance;
On his self-fulfilling judgment day.

Fixed on his own insecurities,
A complex persuasion with endless possibilities;
Fed this ruthless invasion of disregarded privacy;
Destroying his own democracy;
To hide secrets that could bring a country down.

Sickening.

Breeding idiots

Mindless drones, dialling phones.
Eyes glued to shows viewed,
These willing sheep are easy reap
As ratings soar and they want more.

Mindless art, lacking heart,
Innocent guilt is falsely built.
Creating destruction through soulless production,
As listeners soar and they want more.

Dreary eyed and losing pride,
The fleeing heard sees everything blurred,
A clueless reinvention to fund the devils pension.

When everything is one in the same
People, sounds and fashion;
Who is it to blame?

[...]

The ugly twisted soul;
Black heart, suit and hair,
Is he not but fulfilling his role?

The blame lies within,
And my patience razor thin.

You watch and laugh,
At how pathetic they all seem,
Yet they sit and laugh at you,
As you fund their twisted scheme.

Yet you're the first to complain;
When everything you see around,
Looks and sounds the same.

Now we're all just getting bored of everything we once
adored,
It's such a mess and we want less.

Chemical Warfare

Eyes water,
As the air outside turns toxic.
Lungs burn,
Chests collapse under the deadweight
Of unspoken words,
And callous regrets,
Engraved into chest cavities;
Wrenched open for eternal viewing.

Copa

Passion,
Merged in colour,
Drenched in sweat,
After a full-blooded battle;
Leave with no regret.

A carnival of colour,
Enraging a warzone,
This is the result of blood money stolen;
Now we see the seeds they've sown.

The Long Search for Nothing

Traipsing through the hollow shell;
Of an absent suburban dream;
The façade of perfection falls hard.
Smiles no longer bloom here;
Cynicism sets in;
And bears its fruitless teeth.

The haze of mystique;
No longer clouds the judgment of misguided dreamers;
Instead the fog of regret;
Wreaks havoc on these lonely streets;
Even when the sun peeks through;
There is nothing left to do.
But bathe in the wreckage
Of all your broken dreams.

Blind Eye

Six million people persecuted and murdered,
I sit here and hear someone say they probably deserved it?
I feel sick inside.

Who are you to decide who should have lived and who died?

They say general ignorance is bliss,
If that's the case then we face the abyss,
What kind of imbecile could so easily dismiss,
This cataclysmic event that scarred the course of history
But I guess we could talk about something else instead.

Unflattering Words

A sordid criticism is nothing
To be taken lightly, if at all.
What remains is the droll ramblings
Of those whose pens remain untouched
And brains remain unused.

Somewhere out there is an idea.
Where?
I don't think I'll ever know;
But when you find it,
Be gentle.
Because that idea could save your life.

I'll keep writing lines of heresy;
Against your bureaucratic Satanism,
In the hope that you'll one day
Accept my amiable constructivism.

Box of Snakes

A box of snakes is what you make of it,
Could be used for good or evil,
For your wealth or for your giving,
That's completely your decision.

If you try to rid of them,
They'll just come back to bite you.
Do not play with fire;
Or you'll end up getting burnt.

Arrogance

Is it not a dream that conquers us?
A thoughtless portal into your sub-conscience,
This audacious attempt at freedom is consuming reality,
And destroying all you hold dear.

Your skin will writhe in pain,
And the lepers thrive to feast upon your rotting skin,
Only one can save you from this mortal sin,
But when it all goes wrong,
You just blame it on Him.

Commodity

A game controlled by money is no longer a game,
It's a toy.

A toy is not real,
A toy has no emotion,
A toy has no feeling.

If you play too much with a toy; it will break and it will
crumble.

Irreplaceable,
Unfixable,
Unlovable.

We are not the play things of the rich;
We are not customers to be charmed or objects to be sold;
We are people;
We are fans;
And we are angry.

Do not take away our love;
Do not take away our game;
Because when it all goes wrong for you,
And trust me, soon it will,
You'll have no one left to blame.

Tiger

A tiger on a
Mountain rarely smiles for
He can see it all.

Turned to Stone

Hear the swirling roar,
It breaks early morning silence,
The night is no more,
Broken by narcissistic footsteps on lazy stone,
And troubled mortar.

How they moan in displeasure,
At being used in such a way,
A life so unpleasant serves a greater purpose;
And fills a greater canvas.

He grumbles in anger,
But there's nothing he can do.

Dead End Path

Tired heads speak clearer than ever,
Weary eyes and troubled minds,
Scream loudly through the wind.

Hungry,
Alone,
Contemplative.

The condition of all young men trying to find their way in the
world.

Many paths fascinate,
But dead ends block the way.

In the end it matters not what you choose to do;
Because when the bell tolls,
The rich will be as dead as me and you.

Crows

On tenterhooks and crumbling floors,
We walk silently to the mortal grave.
The crow stands watch on heavens hellish gates;
Looking down on us,
Lying in wait,
For us to join him one day.

When our time comes we all run and hide,
Never ready to leave the world behind;
What must the crow think? Sat way up there,
He must be lonely and the world doesn't care.

Nothing

Cave in to nothing, I dare you.
Render me speechless,
Render us worthless,
That's all it comes down to in the end.
Turning something to nothing,
But I think it's nothing to nothing.

Either way, who would know?
I certainly wouldn't.
And in the end, who would care?
I certainly wouldn't.

Hurricanes and Earthquakes

The floor shakes beneath our feet,
Telemetry off the chart,
The damage uncontrollable,
Loss of life severe,
All that becomes clear,
No one can survive here,
And now we can't evacuate,
The rest is up to fate.

They told us it was coming,
Yet you sat and nothing,
Up there in your own fortress,
Of ignorance and disdain.
No water, not a drop, shall pass
Your impenetrable wall.

But be careful now,
Look at the sky;
The eye of the storm is on its way.

Keys

What good is a lock that has many keys?
No good.

It might work for a while,
But eventually,
You'd need a new lock;
One that's right for your key.
I guess some people are never happy.

Opening Eyes

All around me I see people living off greed,
Taking food from the mouths they're meant to feed.
All around me I see people living off war,
Pouring salt in the wounds of those still sore.

All around me I see people living off betrayal,
We are endless victims of a victimless portrayal.
All around me I see people living off lies,
Telling more to get ahead towards the unwinnable prize.

All around me I see people living off crime,
For all that you've stolen, you're wasting your time.

Nothing is reachable in this one-way world,
My broken heart is joylessly unfurled,
In one door and out the other,
Yet I still see people running for cover.

Simplistic Confusion

They say that there are only two things,
That can satisfy any man,
I find that a bit too simplistic.

They say that only sex
And money can make a man happy.
I think they might be wrong.

Never have I met a man
More inclined by sex than solitude.
It seems men only want one thing;
To be left alone.

If it's all so simple,
Why am I struggling
To comprehend if this is even true?
Leave me alone for a minute and I'll tell you.

Sit hand in hand with one song in your heart,
If you can save yourself, at least that's a start.

Battles

Stories of my Existential Life I: The Fear

I hope that I die when I'm tired of life.

I feel so alone; not that I'm lonely,
I'm in a room full of people.
Talking,
Laughing,
Being,
All the things that I am not.

When everyone's gone I'll be on my own;
I'll tell myself, fine, I was always alone.

I get confused sometimes as to what I'm doing here;
I look up not to search but to laugh and to cry;
Out of anger and out of fear.

These people keep yelling and I keep not listening,
Last time I listened I came somehow to cry,
When I try to listen they make the wrong sounds,
Nothing I can do but shy.

I rack my brain in search of truth;
The light makes things darker, not a little a bit clear;
I ask myself why am I human?
And why am I here?

Stories of my Existential Life II: The Nihilist

A man sits swinging his legs on the wooden bridge;
The ageing wood creaks beneath him,
As he shifts awkwardly from side to side;
His face as clear as the sky

The sun bounces from the rooftops,
Illuminating the silent fields below,
The wind blows the blossoming flowers gently;
The silent canal crinkles like paper in the gentle breeze

The scene is picturesque;
But the man has no camera.

He feels no joy, no sadness,
He feels no anger, no calm,
He feels no fear,
He feels nothing.

He is even more alive than you or I?

A solitary child is playing alone,
She smiles toward the man,
Perhaps even she feels pity for him.
I know I would,
I know I do.

Stories of my Existential Life III: Looking Forward

Looking up at the stars,
Never gave me an answer,
I had to look inside myself,
To find what I feared.

Born alone, die alone,
It's the way that we live,
We've all destroyed God,
We just wanted rid.

Now he's left us to die.

Please come back for me.

Detachment

Oh how the colours dance,
In front of the enlightened mind,
Peace eternal,
In the midst of constant flow.

Aware of everything we are;
Deep inside the mind, so far,
A glimpse of freedom;
Shown to me,
Under my very own lonely tree.

Arguing with God

The truth is, it isn't pretty, beautiful or handsome;
It's ugly, like me;
Don't believe me? Come and see.

Sometimes I think about slitting my wrist and ending it all;
Just to see how far my blood shoots up the wall;
It'll be like Jackson Pollock on an acid trip;
Maybe I'll meet God to find out if he exists;
So he can settle all the ethical conflicts,
In my head about taking another man to bed.

I mean, I might as well ask.

Because this argument persists,
We all know how stupid it is,
It's my body and his is his.

Lest Ye Be Judged

Blank stares on grey faces,
Look up to the sky;
And pray,
"Will you save us all today?"
Look and laugh,
In smug condescension,
Nobody is coming soon.

When looking up is all you know;
It becomes harder to let go;
Of everything you once believed;
In place of something new;
But know that nothing's new;
Especially you.

The Woman

My shoulder made of lead,
From memories I've carried all these years,
Nothing needs to be said.
But then again does it ever?
And who is listening anyway?
Nobody ever listens to me
I cry, I beg, I plead!
But nobody ever listens to me.
The fact of the matter is that I would bleed
Before anyone would listen to me;
Yet I still continue talking.

To whom you may ask?
That is the question,
The question I cannot answer.
Yet I still continue talking,
To the woman behind the mask.

The woman stares at me,
I know she's laughing but I do not know why.
Sometimes it seems like she is crying,
But I do not know why.
Maybe I just convinced myself that it was okay to cry;
After all, why should I care who cries?
It's not as though anyone is listening.

Nobody ever listens,
And by then it is too late.

Misplaced

A misplaced soul,
Glides aimlessly,
Through his proverbial hell.

Feet burning
At the thought of flying;
Soaring over this abyss,
And moving on from all of this,
Looking down at the failing,
And screaming,
"I'm free!"

Again he wakes;
Cold sweat burns his cracked skin,
And frail mind.

Never further from freedom,
Than this transparent cage,
A private island;
Encasing violence;
Screaming in fits of rage,
**"If this is living,
Then I don't want to live!"**

twenty One Pilots

And from above I hear the sound;
Of twenty one pilots,
Crashing down to earth,
Guiding their planes into darkness;
And when this pen falls silent,
In the middle of the night;
I hear them screaming.

Begging not to live;
But not to die;
Only to find comfort in knowing;
That everything real must end.

And until now,
It never occurred to me why;
Twenty one pilots,
Were flying twenty one planes.

Reprise

And because I've found what I thought I'd lost;
There is a war going on inside,
As my heart and brain collide.

Roll back the clock,
Pretend that time hasn't changed a thing,
I am where I was,
Nothing bad has happened yet,
Nor will it ever again;
Where joy once lived,
There was only pain.

Drawing Blanks

Heartbeat racing;
Throbbing veins;
Drenched in sweat;
The fear takes over.

Time is going slower but the world beings to spin;
Red mist descends over silent ridges,
Eyes roll and tongues wag,
Lights flicker on and off,
Blood is in the air.

Faint.
Fall.
The only truth is in our veins.

Impregnable

A thousand lights to blur the racing mind,
Nothing is what it seems,
Painted in chaos,
The air is thick and heavy,
Silent screams from fallen angels,
Ring loudly on softened ears.

Suffocating in heat;
Like tar on the lungs;
I soldier on through the jungle.

Determined to find peace,
Through the clouds of cars I see;
A simple space beneath,
This humble bodhi tree.

Classic Signs of Ageing

The mood once more is sombre;
The air is filled with hatred,
Befouling every night.

I'm caught in solitary moments;
Of remembering that I'm human;
Our suffering and the plight.

This what we are;
It is what we have become.

We are aware of what we are;
We know what's coming next.

This is a classic sign of ageing;
The whole world is burning slowly;
We are the only warriors;
And our time is rapidly fading.

Love Letters

Dockyard

Swaying in a sympathetic wind;
Rusted homes of former glory;
Sit lonely on the shore,
Their hero's stories heard no more.

Ramblings of an Inuit

A frozen wasteland so beautiful;
Paint upon the blank canvas;
The finest gift of all.
Look out for miles,
The twinkle of the snow,
Lights up all the humble smiles.

Night is closer than day,
Sky alight with eyes,
That capture a thousand wanderers;
In awe of something special,

The ice desert stands alone,
And brings us all to tears,
Magnifying the intensity,
Of the brilliant daylight,
Illuminating fields of white,
And sea of blue.

A Reflection

Chocolate brothels on streets of common vice;
Lead each dreary eyed man;
Stumbling down paths of sloth and gluttony;
For we are all willing victims here;
A timid love affair with the richer things in life;
I will never be the same again.

The city has no secrets;
Holds no trembling fear;
A simple place that lives so quietly,
It comes alive under light;
And through the biting cold;
Although the cold trials me;
There is no question;
That this is where I want to be;
In this grand, old city.

Semper Invicta

A beautiful city,
Haunted by memories of blood and loss,
New life towers high above the old,
Into the sky.

Hear the melodies of Chopin;
That the softest angels sing;
Here in Warsaw, hope is king;
In the city that never dies.

Market Town

Hustling,
Bustling,
Food papers rustling.

The invading air is oh so pleasant;
Heaven scent,
By Ambrosia's fair hand.
Travel stall to stall,
Life's simple pleasures call,
Out to a starving wanderer.

Take your pick;
It's easy to get lost in it.

The mind flows like wine,
As my lips begin to purse, my feet carry me home;
That first taste; utterly divine.

How can it be;
That in a city almost devoid of pleasure;
Its finest hidden simple treasure;
Lies not in a famous cathedral, abbey or shop?
Instead it's underneath a simple bridge,
That the world does stop.

One Early Morning

A thin veil covers the glistening horizon,
Tumultuous landscape frail in the early light,
Cold air penetrated by the warm sun,
Peeking its head in trepidation through dusty morning clouds.

The luminous technicolor sky,
Lights the gloomy path with three colours at once;
The fiery black lights the way;
Brilliant orange fights back.

A deathly blue lingers,
Natural light so artificial on this perfect day.

Down pours the rain,
Treading lightly on the gentle ebb of the twinkling river;
Swaying in the gentle wind,
Here comes the fearsome sky again.

The King of Belgium

Golden throws on threads divine;
A blend so precious,
This treasure of mine.

The glimmer of your hair;
Matches the beautiful décor,
Which with the world I shall not share.

For we're nothing to all we see;
But in our perfect world,
We live in luxury.

Grote Markt

Winding cobbles filled with excitement and flowing with
beer;
Lead to that majestic place,
Alive with colour buoyant with murmurs,
About the magnificence of those ancient towers,
Watching down on us all;
Smiling.

This is the only place to be.

A Whirlwind Romance

Young love is nothing new,
Especially when she is as pretty as you.
Full of life, full of soul,
Always talking, breathing in my ear on my Sunday stroll,
Some people say our love is strange.

The city that always sleeps.
The sleeping giant that lurks in.
The urban rainforest.

She is beautiful and I am not,
At least that's what I've been told.

I've never felt more at home.

Ghost Town

The lights ablaze with neon glow;
Pebbles, dusted with ice;
Frozen wasteland;
Industrial heaven;
Not a soul to die here,
This is the life of the party.

You speak in tongues,
For all else is foreign;
There's a ghost in this town,
Its name long forgotten;

He looks like you and talks like you;
You swear you've never seen him;
No one here knows your name.

Time to go;
Time to live.

British Summer Time

Summer walks on fresh shores,
Greet the new light,
Revelling in the gentle flight;
Of a thousand birds,
Dance to the echo,
Of an ocean's thunderous roar.

Children play so merrily,
On the pebbled beach,
Oblivious to the world,
And here I sit,
Much closer to the world,
Than I could ever admit.

That Mysterious Woman

I took a long walk today,
Down that long ramshackled old street,
Hidden from everyone that I could still see.
The flickering neon and restless candles
Seemed to guide me,
To that old café that I love so dear.
(The one with the apricot pastry)

The weary baker, who recognized me by now
Called out to me, he said
'Monsieur, what do you think of Paris?'
'Paris', I replied;
'Pourquoi elle est magnifique'
He chuckled
'Then why do you always look so sad?'
I chuckled;
'Because she is so beautiful.'

He said he did not understand;
So I spoke again.
He chuckled.
'I understand not your meaning.'
I laughed again,
I explained, partly in English,
Partly in French, but wholly in Truth;
'How can one be happy,
When she is so beautiful and one is not?'

Alas, he did not have an answer.

The Cafe

Winding roads of bliss,
Temples of the soul,
Feast the senses.

The sights bathed in the glorious lights,
The smells,
And their enchanting spells;
The sounds,
Of eager feet on medieval grounds.

Shops cling together,
Vendors wail,
Patrons bustle,
Sit by the roadside and let the world pass by.

What'll it be sir?
"Café-Vermouth"
And one for the lady too.

Grand Old Lady

Deafening drums roll and heads go silent;
No thoughts needed,
Just the fear;
The expectation;
The deadly anticipation.

Nerves are shredded,
Stomachs tight,
The drum roll ends,
It's time to fight.

A hero's welcome;
A villain's snarl;
The street roars,
Expectation gone,
It's time to play,

Game on.

The English Way

Nervous eyes catch a glance;
Across the crowded plain;
We're just two simple strangers waiting for a train.

The battle looms as our chariot beckons;
The war is won in those vital seconds;
Shaking madly side to side;
Apologising awkwardly as our bodies collide.

Steel on steel,
Flesh on flesh.

The calming sound,
Of being caught in a jungle,
On the London Underground.

Fields of Kent

The red mist descends;
No one knows where it ends.

But the sky is grey;
As this gentle day comes crashing into view;
The silent rolling hills pass on the haunting chills,
Birds cry out;
In hopeful doubt;
The day begins again.

Flowers perk and raise their heads;
A whirlpool of powerful blues and brilliant reds.

Picture perfect scenery;
Holds lust and powerful mystery.

All aglow in mid-morning sun,
The humble fields of England;
A green and mighty kingdom;
Sit silently tonight,
Precious in the fading light.

Another day has ended.

Old Wien

Up here;
So peaceful above the world,
Watching the city,
As it unfurled beneath my feet.

On the horizon;
I see the sunset borders far and wide,
Where Heaven and Earth collide,
Reach out and touch God as he looks down on this fair city.

This is His country;
For so long I struggled;
But now he's coming back to me again,
Thanks to old Wien.

Waterways

The deep winding alleys of ancient times,
Whisper secret tongues to lovers.
The Venice of Flanders stirs in the silent night;
Inhale her beauty.

A cacophony of the senses;
Bring humble men to their knees.
In a town so quaint,
Beneath the world,
It's here we wait;
To be rescued from this pleasant hell.

Where the Mountains Meet the Sea

Beating sun warms my humble skin;
The brilliant daylight falls down upon its garden;
Rays filled with muse caress a lonely traveller;
Luscious mountains stand proud looking down on a vibrant metropolis;
Inflicting awe and wonder on simple humble patrons.
Crisp air breathes life into tired lives;
Crunching sand stands firm beneath exhausted feet;
Jagged coasts impeccable.

The freedom,
White and blue;
Gaze upon their splendour,
For me it's nothing new.
Suburban jungles collide with dense fields of brown and green;
City sounds fill the ears,
People dance to their powerful rhythm,
They come alive in summer.

No division or unity;
Protected by their brother,
Standing tall,
High in the trees away from it all;
Take heavens ascent and meet the royal call.

Crusaders come from all around to see this famous bay of dreams;
Where the mountains meet the sea.

Days End

On modern streets of ancient times,
We walk gently,
Through our simple lives.

We're not alone,
Dusty windows offer portals into secrecy;
Another world lies beyond;
The last charade of privacy.

Slanting roads to hidden treasures,
A town of fools;
Hides simple pleasures.

Dig up the roots of any man and you will find,
Something he can never leave behind.

This ghastly town clings to me;
In my shame,
For all to see.

But sitting by the waterside,
Staring out into the vast temptation of the sea;
I get the feeling,
That nowhere can ever mean as much,
As this place does to me.

Montmartre

Down the rolling hills;
Cobbled streets bathe in cold artificial glow,
Thinly leafed trees,
Barely covers a busker's lonely song.

Twisting cafes harbour poet's dreams,
Artistic souls are destined to go unnoticed here it seems;
The views are stunning;
Salesman cunning.

The beating heart of Paris stirs,
Nothing ordinary occurs in this gentle lovers quarter;
Lose yourself to find yourself,
On the mount of rolling hills.

In Critique

Picturesque but fading,
A crumbling ruin;
Holds faint hopes of rejuvenation;
Estranged awards and prizes offer little compensation.

For this ghost of a city,
Haunted by false glory,
Scarred by its own vanity,
Lays destined for dormancy.

Not asleep but comatose,
How Arnold would wince,
If the cities famous prince,
Could see you now.

Sitting in London

The clatter of hooves,
Disturbs the peaceful ambience;
Of this pleasant day.
        My concrete chair,
        Is fair game;
        To busy passing souls.

The Kings Canal (Chao Phraya)

In rustic glory she dances;
Meandering like a devils angel;
Formed on former lands of gold and green;
Weaved with promise, life and hope;
Now she carries land.

Filled with extravagant and modern fare;
With which the land can barely cope;
Yet deep amongst this unnatural jungle;
She passes through,
Carving wide the dense new land.

With the splendour of old;
The splendour of the mighty;
The splendour of the grand.

Left on King Street

A biting wind whips,
Through my ragged hair,
A lonely kid in the city,
Looking for nothing but
Looking forward to everything.

People in suits hurry by,
Setting off for the day,
Unaware that I don't belong here;
Yet,
A million miles from home,
I've never fit in more.

As I turn left on King Street;
I close my eyes,
My world spins but everything stops;
A shop window captures my reflection,
Eye-catching imperfection.

I hurry on,
Pushing past a lonely kid with ragged hair;
Standing dazed in the street;
I have no time for him,
And he has no time for me;
My new suit and I have places to be.

Belvedere

Where I once blossomed,
Is now where I die.
The cool air outside,
And the sun in my eyes;
Only hide the fact;
That now I'm dead inside.

Prater

As I watch the lights,
Swirl out through the dark,
Upon the Sandman's quest;
I do embark,
As I look out upon,
Old Prater Park.

A swirling dream takes hold;
I dream of those colours;
Faded blue and dazzling gold;
And with sluggish lark,
I look out in joy upon,
Old Prater Park.

Painted Hallways (Apartment 18)

Haunted feet on creaking floors,
Whisper in the dead of night.
The moans and groans of the old mistress;
Stir sleeping patrons.

Her spine creaks,
As she sleeps another night;
Beneath these haunted feet.

Albert Street

As cars rushed by on Albert Street;
The earth began to stir beneath my feet.

Although my life turned upside down;
On that street of red and brown;
I found myself
With no-one else;
On this plain so far from home;
Yet I've never felt less alone.

Oh, how I lived on Albert Street.

Pastry

As I sit trying to consume,
An item of food that was not;
In a million years,
Designed to be eaten on public transport.

I sit and wonder;
Am I *that guy* on the bus?

Or tram in this case.

Crumbs caught in my overflowing beard;
Sticky contents of the aforementioned apricot pastry
Dribbling down my chin;
Scrambling aimlessly for napkins,
In long forgotten pockets.

I sit and wonder;
Am I *that guy* on the bus?

[...]

But then it occurred to me;

If I were *that guy* on the bus;
Would it really bother me,
If I were?
Would I even be worrying about whether I was?
Maybe I am crazier now;
For writing this than I ever was before.

Or maybe;
Like so many over times in life,
Just maybe;
I am just overthinking this.

It was a nice pastry though.

Calm Amongst the Chaos

Buzzing lights;
Sinful delights;
Pushed and pulled,
In crowds of wonder.

Sweat dripping;
Hands tingling;
Surrounded by ghosts,
But a touch away.

A neon jungle,
That never sleeps,
Has taken firm grasp of me.

Yet here we stand,
Upon this busy night;
A private heaven,
Of hellish treats;
A welcome slice,
Of calm amongst the chaos.

The Night Train to Rangoon

Dreary eyes flicker under the gentle rushing light;
Heads drift away,
And the train marches into the night.

Chariots of steel on polished rails carry us home;
The tip-tapping of children's fingers on wooden seats;
Distract the last weary eyes from closing.

An unassuming whistle rouses fallen eyes,
Before they drift away again;
I, for one, cannot sleep tonight.

The dusty window holds my gaze;
Staring out over the lonely midnight landscape,
Contemplating the existence of this never ending world.

As I began to wonder for the thousandth time;
A sound begins to catch my ear;

Tip
Tap
Tip
Tap

My thoughts are lost inside my head, never to be found;
At least for now, this train is homeward bound.

City of Pride

A city by the river,
Living so proud;
To the glory of music,
A blessing endowed.

In from the cold,
Boats sail in ancient ports;
A city united by grief,
Divided by sports.

A heated rivalry,
In colours red or blue;
Defines a city,
Where the liver bird flew.

Introspections

Avoiding the Void

There is a deepening void within;
And I hear the darkness calling.

It beckons in the night like a haunting temptress;
Pulling in the weakest man to kneel before her;
There is no escape from this mighty chasm,
A bottomless pit that steals the breath of life.

Here within these walls there is nothing;
Not a hint of life nor happiness to be found,
Yet after all this is home and I am truly comfortable,
Sinking is easier than fighting.

You won't realise until it's too late;
That this was never the home for you.

The Bear Pit

The bloody pit beckons;
A foul stench of death haunts the tainted air;
Terror reigns on the so-called golden fields;
Blood diamonds stolen by the undeserving;
The only blood spilt is that which is replaceable.

Outside the pit is organised hell;
Inside the pit is heavenly carnage;
Introverted personalities intimidate my captors;
But they do not intimidate me.

I am hunted, I am free.

The Hunted

It seems, for great shame
That life is passing me by;
"Oh life, thou art failing me."

We live in hypocrisy of privacy,
Because we have none anymore;
Yet we hide ourselves away;
It's not just you and me,
More like everyone you see.

We are being hunted,
For what films we like;
For which music we listen to;
And which foods we eat at 2am.

If knowledge is power,
Why aren't I king?

Life isn't passing by me;
It's passing right through me.

The War

Light-headed dreams are never easy;
They taunt the lonely man,
The light makes him queasy;
But the dark makes him sick,
From the nightmares it holds.

Slumber takes its grip,
She shines through in her darkness,
He quivers,
Sun kissed skin haunted by ruby lips;
Sandy hair devastated with a crimson smile;
Burning blue eyes gladly pierce me;
Uneasy stares beckon forth,
A haunting whisper so seductive;
Bringing fond memories of a devilish nightmare.

You lay in wait for me to sleep;
My life is surrendered to a spectre;
No food passes these lips of yours;
I've surrendered to you.

I know I've seen you before,
This is not over.

[...]

The beautiful air of death hangs like a cloud,
Over this marriage bed;
Gone but never left,
The dream is over,
I'm coming for you.

Another tedious day draws to an end;
Lay down in bed and rest my eyes;
Where is my ghostly mistress tonight?
The love that I despise.
She skulks alone in the background hidden from sight;
I tell myself it's just a dream,
But that gave me such a fright.

Eyes flatter to deceive,
In a manner most unknown;
They fool me once as she speaks
In that haunted calming tone.
She glides across the dusty floor,
To whisper softly to me;
The only thing you need to know,
In your dreams I'll always be.

I awoke.

The music blares all around;
Visions of beauty dance through the night,
Dancing so gracefully to the intoxicating sound.

[...]

Tonight she wants to see me;
To stare me dead in the face;
So, running I come,
Destined for her warm embrace;
My fingers go numb,
And my heart starts to race;
My head starts to wonder,
Is this the end of the chase?

As I lean in for a kiss I see
A single tear in her eye;
She says it's for me,
Silently we cry;
Before she whispers again;
This must be goodbye.

She waves,
Before turning the saddest of turns,
It all becomes clear,
That this man never learns.

My dreams are not my own tonight;
Visions of tantalizing angel wings on golden sheets of former
anguish;
Stir this fatal sleep.

[...]

But as I rub dry eyes I find myself awake;
Outside of your control,
The fragrance of your beauty can tempt this man no more.

Staring out the window,
Overlooking the destitution that this war has brought;
A lonely figure sits,
Facing the wall,
On that frail old park bench;
Sandy hair blowing in the wind.

Mantra

Don't be your best self in the hope
That it will be good enough for someone else.
Be your best self,
To show everyone else how good you can be.
And when you finally find someone
Who is worth you being your best self for;
Don't romanticise them.

They're not perfect,
And in imperfection lies true happiness.

Home Comforts

Home is far too comfortable,
Yet comfort is our greatest fear,
And the comfort of home is overwhelming.
It's been a long time coming,
But now I have to leave once more.
I'd die just to feel alive again.

Not Now

They didn't cut off my hands,
But I feel like I can't touch anything anymore.

They didn't cut off my ears;
But I feel like I can't hear anyone anymore.

Is this the way you're meant to feel?

It's been so long that I just don't know anymore.
How am I supposed to feel?

In a world that doesn't make sense,
There's nothing you can do for me,
Because you don't need me anymore.

I feel like I've been away for years,
But it's only been days;
I feel like I have no one,
When I've just pushed them away.

Man in the Mirror

I look in the mirror hung up on the door,
I say pleased to meet you, how do you do?
To the person I've not seen before.

You look like someone I used to know;
But I thought that he had died years ago.
Or at least I hoped he had.

It turns out that he never goes away.

A Kick in the Face for Hope

I've been dragged to the brink,
And brought right back again.
There's no shortcut to heaven,
But I thought I'd try anyway.

You never know,
Traffic might have been light that day.
Death is a natural part of life;
So I thought I'd get it out of the way.

You knocked on the door,
And I said I was busy;
All you wanted to know was what I wanted for my dinner.

Majesty

If I could be anyone; I think I'd be a bird.
I could fly anywhere I wanted to,
Whenever I wanted to;
Rather than listening to the bus timetables;
Which seem hell bent on going at times
That I don't want them to.

Birds fly majestically,
I wait impatiently.

What's the point in walking anywhere?
When there are things to take us there.
A bird wouldn't have these problems,
Now you see,
Why it would be good to be a bird,
And not a person.
Although I suspect that I stopped
Being one of those a long time ago.

Do birds dream?
If not then I'd make an excellent bird;
I gave that up years ago too.

Missing

I wish people would stop
Telling me to plan for the future,
'You must care about the future!'
Why?
I might not even be around in the future.

Definitely not the way I'm going anyway.
I barely care about the present.

So why should I care about the future,
When the future doesn't care about me?

Storm in a Teacup

I hear the noise outside again,
The howling winds, the pouring rain.
It lashes down, innate, ferocious, without pity;
It beats the ground with an unrivalled ferocity.
The winds howl,
The sky is foul.

The sound grows louder by the second,
On the horizon does thunder beckon.
I love the sound.
I want the sound.
People say that they hate something that I have found.

So calming, so assuring.
Are they lying?
Or am I crazy?

The Clown

I always thought I'd be the first to leave this town,
This dead rubber, backwater town.

I had plans to leave, to fly;
I wonder why
I never saw them through.

I always thought I'd be the first to leave,
But now I'm stuck here and time is turning quicker.
My time is up and I'm still stuck;
Destined to never fly the nest.

I am the ostrich that dared to dream.

I never wanted to be an ostrich,
How funny;
Maybe I am the clown, the sad clown.

Am I the sad clown in the sad town,
With the sad frown looking down,
At everything I wanted to be and wondering
'Where did it all go wrong?'
I am the clown who knew it was okay to be sad.

Do I have to be what everyone wants me to be?
After all I'm only me,
And I am free.
I still have time,
We all have time.

The Day I Died

I remember the day I died.

The birds cried out for me;
Half in pain,
Half in sorrow.

Like me, they fall to the earth flat on their face.
Will this feeling come again tomorrow?
Or will I shake its eerie grace?

Do you remember the day that I died?

Of course you don't,
Of course you won't.
Ignorance is bliss,
Just like a devil's kiss.

You said you'd never die,
As long as I'm alive.
Now I see that for what it was;
A filthy, rotten lie.

I wish I didn't remember the day I died.

How to Accept a Compliment

Pretend not to be riddled with crippling insecurity.
Smile politely to mask feelings of vulnerability.
Say thank you;
Fight the urge to disagree;
Walk away.

Burnt Tongues

And I'm tired of life again,
I don't know where to begin,
Just go from the start,
Where it all fell apart,
Can you point out where it will end?

Nothing is as simple as it seems;
Depths of despair unexplored;
Teeming with beings unknown.
In the dark I cower
From my own mind;
And its despicable unearthly power.

A road ahead is bleak,
My tongue can no longer speak;
Burnt at both ends,
And buried by an all consuming hubris;
Whimpers roll from charred flesh;
Passive aggressive slurs,
In contempt of content souls;
Run amok in fields of red and grey.

Trees

Somewhere, in the trees;
Stands a lonely figure, as lonely as me;
Silent, he stands for all to see.

A selfish man who stands alone amongst the trees;
Waiting for the wind to tell a story.

He himself is now the story unknowingly;
One final breath,
He waits for death;
It may never come,
But to him he is already dead.

Empty

I thought I knew what empty felt like but as I sit here in a
pitch black room without walls of solace, a glass of scotch
stirring in one hand and a cigarette burning out in the other, I
feel like a bottomless pit.

Dealing With Rejection by Proxy (If Only..)

You smile,
Telling yourself you're okay,
As perfection fades away before you;

Life together,
With one foot into the sunset that you hoped could be yours;
But sadly will never be.

Why is it always me?
Why is it *never* me?

Fog

And suddenly,
It comes again;
The weight of the fog;
Crushing the smallest of dreams;
Extinguishing every spark of life.

The weary lose their way;
Sigh no more;
For my lungs have collapsed;
Under the weight of the fog.

There is silence in the world
And all is wrong;
False smiles hide suffocation,
Through a veil of curious design;
This is how the world ends,
Bathed in darkness.

Break

The nearest dose of reality
That I have in my life is
That moment I dream of us
Together, always happy inside a mind
That never is.

This what I've become,
This is what I am.

A Letter to Myself Ten Seconds Ago

You arrogant self centred waste of space, yes I'm talking to you;
What gives you the right to blame other people for your own shortcomings?

People are not objects to be moulded and manipulated;
They have their own minds, feelings and thoughts;
You are not the centre of everything, as much as you'd like to be.

Nobody needs to hear anything negative that you've got to say;
What gives you the right to say anything negative about anyone in the first place?
In fact, why do you even have so much to be negative about?

Your life is a gift, and a pretty decent one at that.
Stop whinging.
Pull yourself together.
Apologise.
Move on.
Grow up.

Sincerely,
Me

The Sparrow

There's a sparrow on my windowsill,
I don't know what it wants.

I look at its cold, dead eyes,
And I think that it doesn't want anything
But to annoy me.

It taps:

Once,
Twice,
Thrice.

I open the window;
It flies in and circles above my head.

How rude; I thought,
I ask it further questions,
Yet still it does not reply.

It swoops upon my shoulder,
And there it sits quite still.
It makes me feel much older,
Than people ever will.

Proverb

A man who never has his heart broken is a cynic;
A man who has his heart broken once is a learner;
A man who has his heart broken twice is a lover;
A man who has his heart broken more than three times is a
fool.

I guess you could say I'm learning?

Drawn

I hate being drawn,
For it is not a pretty picture,
Especially when it does not concern me.

Death is an ugly mistress
Who paints no worse a picture;
But she will paint us all one day.
Some soon,
Some far,
But you cannot run away.

She paints with a single colour.

This Poem Has No Title and No Meaning

She brings me back from the brink,
Reason is dead
But love
Is alive.
All I wanted was someone to hear me,
And now all I want is to die.

No wonder people leave me.

C'est la Vie

People say that I'm miserable all the time, but I'm not.
I am happy sometimes;
It's just that when I am happy;
I don't talk to people about it because then
I would be sad again.

Empathy

If it feels like I don't care;
I've got no problem being able to share that I don't;
I don't care if you think that it's not fair;
You think it's fair that I have to tear out my fucking hair?
Just to get where you are all the way up there;
On top of your high horse.

Nothing feels the same anymore,
That's because nothing is the same as it was before;
Back before anyone ever saw,
That there might be something wrong going on inside my head.

And I was much more comfortable,
Before someone tried to define the fact that I might not be able,
To feel empathy for another;
And I knew that I had a tendency to display an inability;
To communicate with one or the other.

Read between the lines, you could learn a thing or two.
Yet we're all still terrified.

Ghosts

There are chains around my throat;
Forged in regret, rusted with the sands,
Not yet eroded;
Hidden in plain sight.

Twisted by the love of hate,
Suffocating the truth;
One too many times cold dead hands pull me down,
And wrap the chains around my neck;
Their fury, tight

They strangle;
Squeeze;
A vengeful bite.

When the chains come off I shall be free,
But they will still be there in spirit;
Pulling around my neck,
Dangling, in the breeze.

Dreams

When is a dream no longer a dream?
If nothing seems real and we've seen everything before.

When nothing is new and real life is a blur;
We live out a déjà vu,
Just to pass the time;
Before we all curl up and die.

It's not pleasant,
It's not pretty,
It's life.
Sleep tight.

In Homage

Matador

Clear the way for the new man in town;
He holds his head high and dreams of success,
Neigh; envisions the future.

Pride emblazoned on his mighty chest;
He carries expectation on his back;
Falling upwards never looked so easy.

Smiles all around;
The grass is greener no more.
Right here;
Right now;
Is the place to be.

Let the defiant trumpets sound;
The bull charges once more;
He seems so helpless, alone
Held off with guile and wit;
By the matador unknown.

To him that visions of red;
Will give way to the visions of blue that dance in his head.

The Race

From the lifeless wreckage;
The choking engine sputters into life;

Coughing.
Purring.
Roaring.

The engine turns;
And the machine begins to roll;

Unstoppable.
Unflappable.
Untouchable.

The adrenaline is pumping,
Waiting is no more, excitement building;
Everything we've been waiting for.

King of Nowhere

Sitting by the window, you're wondering;
Why am I God's leader?

Proclaim your prophecy of sanity and reason;
Servants pin you down;
Reality beings to strike;
The pills have saved your life but they no longer work.

A bitter taste left behind
In a mouth so dry;
It burns like deadwood in the desert sun;
Pull the plug and let the king die with dignity.

You were told you are the king of nowhere;
But really, in your heart,
You are the king of everywhere.

Raymond

Urban rhythms stir the gentle soldier;
Footsteps on hollow cobbles;
Harsh stone dressed in subtle leather;
Echo around his solitary room;
Anxious dogs bark to tranquil owners;
Just another urban day to treasure.

The sun penetrates his dusty window;
Rag curtains do little to shut out intruders;
He stirs again;
The pillow is an uncomfortable mistress;
He used to love this place;
But this is now and that was then.

It used to smell like home once;
Before he was silently bitten,
By that dreadful homesick curse;
Utopia is beautiful,
And everything's the same here;
Yet somehow slightly worse.

Comfort

Water deep;
Fills up slowly;
I can feel the warmth now.

A warm embrace from an old friend
Long lost;
My happy heart can breathe once more,
The deepest sigh of joy;

And just like that
All is well again.

Nelson, Madiba

The dark reveals true light,
Step forward luminescent;
Through courage, strength and fight;
Guide us home.

**Uyindoda emadodeni
Kuwe Imvula iyana endlini
Enkosi kakhuli, Madiba
Ndiyakuthanda**

In Earnest

Stumbling through a drunken haze;
On these lazy Parisian days;
A lonely soul;
Out for his weekly Sunday stroll;
He marauds the cobbled Latin streets;
Yearning for his mistress' sheets.

He staggers towards Saint-Sulpice;
Seeking peace,
From the voices in his mind;
Scared of what he'll find;
No peace is found;
Homeward bound.

There outside sits a lonely mirror;
Through the mist his face is clearer than it ever was before;
Paris has lost its allure;
And without doubt;
He knows he must get out.

The Night

The golden silence of the night was broken only by the sound of my own footsteps. It assured me that I was the only certainty in an uncertain world. If there is nothing but me then I am happy in my own company, as anyone should be. But as I walked the streets, disillusioned with everything I knew about myself, I knew I was alone. Entire worlds crumbled around me as I stood still waiting for the bus, her words still ringing in my ears. It wasn't me, it was anybody else, as it was and always will be. Everything has an expiration date, I just didn't realise mine was already up.

For Jamie

Abundant creativity lights up the darkest room,
Every day is a chance to start anew,
Paint a picture with your words,
Write a beautiful melody,
Let your pictures speak a thousand words.

Trust yourself for no one knows you better;
Aim not to succeed but never to quit;
And give nothing but your best.

Be courageous, be true;
Most importantly, be you.

Wanderer

Tired feet hug the cobbled path;
Dreary eyes trouble party makers;

Laughter.

Weariness takes hold and on trudges the faceless man,
Tired of life;
Haunted by the darkness in the city of light;
No room for the stranger in a city that raised him;
Held in contempt by a city that owns him;
The faceless man is tired of life.

Attired in grey;
He walks alone;
All night and all day in a city that broke him;
The faceless man is tired of life.

That all ends today;
A gin soaked anger grips like a vice;
He screams out in despair,
Not once.. but twice.

The end is coming quickly;
It's something too familiar;
Slips;
Stumbles;
Falls.

[...]

The cold cobbled path holds no solace for his old weary
head;
He will be going home tonight;
For the streets no longer shelter our weary, broken, faceless
man
From the city that stole his fight.
Where are you going tonight?
The world is so big, so wide;
There is almost nowhere to hide;
The faceless man walks alone in the night.

These are his streets,
The streets that made him hold no grudge;
He may hate a city of fallen angels but still he returns here,
Time after time;
Year after year.

The charmless wife puts out his dinner;
She knows not where he is;
No longer does she care;
The faceless man is with his mistress tonight.

She does not know the woman whose husband she stole;
A city more beautiful than he;
But with an ugly soul,
She is magnificent no more.

Blurred

Your name's Blurryface and I care what you think.

A mirage of emotions anchored in loneliness,
Projected onto strangers with no face;
Blurred in the passing,
I'm searching for the truth;
My feelings aloof,
Hiding away in fright;
Of bubbling to the surface,
And burning in your divine delight.

You're name's Blurryface and I care what you think;
Do you care what I think?

Back at the Ball Game

The scoreboard reads:

Bottom nine.
2 out;
3 on.

"Batter up!" comes the shout,

Way back in the stands sits a child effervescent with joy;
His father beside him speaks to him softly;
Close your eyes and think,
That could be me.

The roar of the throbbing crowd longing for victory
Seats teeming with fans
Some sad with worry, some happy with glee.

The scuffing of shoes,
The clearing of throats,
The build up to when pandemonium ensues.

That old smell of peanuts,
The roll of the organ,
The batter steps up to take his cuts.

He steps up to the plate,
Breathes; and takes it all in
He closes his eyes and thinks to himself;
Why me and not him?

The Smoke

Smoke billows down,
In streams of ghastly terror,
The fire has spread,
Disaster ahead.

Tears cannot steady the vast flames;
Onlookers rush helplessly;
Smoke gets in your eyes;
Thick clouds cover helpless skies;
We shall not forget what happened here.

Years later;
On a tragic second stage;
There is still no comfort to be found,
In memoriam of the day,
That words can't fix;
The catastrophe of the fifty-six.

Tito

We find strength in the strangest places;
Sometimes in words,
Sometimes in games,
As long as we're surrounded by familiar faces.

For all to see;
We stand tall in battle,
And all take strength from you,
Our revered Marquis.

Never forget;
That our time is not set;
Not enough time with so much to do,
But most importantly,
We will never forget you.

Twenty-Five

Twenty-five years have passed;
Still we're haunted by the ghosts of the past;
But the smiles of justice are coming at last.

We shall lay them to rest,
In the wake of relentless protest;
And tears fall on banners of hope;
Because the city can cope.

With all the lies that you throw,
About that fateful day;
Twenty-five years ago.

Ninety Six

A thousand lies were told,
About those who can't grow old.
Justice never rests and truth is always found,
The screaming of the kop in that famous old ground,
Will always be for justice to be done,
The battle for their loved ones has only just begun.

United we stand in times of great appal,
We put aside things as futile as football.

The dead had their voice taken,
We tried our best to bring it back,
And now the country's shaken;
To its bloody, rotten core.

In times of dark there's always light,
And for the good hard working people,
There's meaning in the fight,
For those who sobbed within that famous steeple.

Walk on with love and hope in your hearts,
Forever remembered within these parts.

And now I make a promise to you;
Those who lost their lives that day,
Because united we stand, red and blue;
Someone soon will pay.

Temporary Lover

Winter nights come round again;
So cold and lonely;
Yet filled with joy.
Hearing running water trickle;
Sends shivers down the spines;
Hairs on end,
The mirror, pointlessly fickle.

Biting air and whistling wind;
It catches on the lips,
And inside the gentle ear;
It grasps so tightly;
Gasping, shaking,
Like a lover's touch without the charm.

A darling night,
With love so tight,
Is not at all too wrong.

My love affair with summer waned,
And or some reason unexplained;
I ask,
Winter won't you come again?

A year is far too long.

Beautiful Stranger

Beautiful stranger;
A blank silhouette on the greyed canvas of a broken heart;
Dancing three times fast,
The lines are blurred between present and past.

Pride cast aside,
An unwanted spectre always looking over the shoulder,
My window is open but nobody can see in;
Nor can I see out.

It serves no purpose other than to protect a façade;
The façade of solitude;
A violent island behind my eyelid,
From which there is no escape.

Oh, beautiful stranger. What have you done?

A Frightful Magnetism

Desire etched across your face as it burns onto mine;
A drive within that closes the widest gaps;
Passion the magnet that pulls,
Two poles from polar opposites,
Closer than they've ever been.

On intimate midnight pixels do their futures rest;
Stuck together in perfect magnetism;
Attracted like a moth to the flame.

Desire burning bright,
Finally, a light;
For these midnight lovers tonight.

Moon Girl

If you were ever unloved before,
You'll never know a love like this.

Craving an embrace that will never come;
A seldom glance to get lost in,
Will have to satisfy this hungry soul.

Coy, I smile;
Hoping that my longing reflects in your beauty;
As your beauty has reflected on me.

Forever lost amongst the stars;
That lurk behind the demure smile,
Which emblazons all that is so far away,
And unattainable.
But behind my wishful thinking;
Lies complete ruin.

To even write this down;
Is one small step for man.
But man, I really want her.

Listen & Learn

No tolerance for ignorance;
Destroying our collective innocence;
No justice for systemic corruption,
And I do apologize for the interruption,
To your regularly scheduled programming.

But this is a matter of life or death,
As yet another takes their final breath.
There are no more fun and games,
Just say their fucking names,
And start to listen closely.

Can You?

I can breathe, can you?
So stand back, listen and learn;
I can't breathe, can you?

Simply Confused

I don't understand the world anymore;
We live on an empty shell;
Drained by greed;
Emptied in the name of technological advance.

The world is getting smaller indeed;
A world in need of reform;
Built on a society formed by arms;
Not reaching out.

Enforcing the peace with their cold demeanour;
Holding out a Trident,
To rule over mortal slaves;
We are inconceivably unimportant in their eyes.

We are angry;
But we have no voice;
The freedom to express crushed under heavy hands.

Those same hands that we need to haul us from the gutter;
But push us down at every chance;
No progress until unity.

We are angry;
But we have no voice;
I don't understand the world anymore.

The Beginning of the End

The Letter

My dear, I'm sorry.

I'm sorry for everything I did to ruin this;
I'm sorry for that stupid kiss;
I'm sorry for walking out;
I'm sorry for breeding doubt.

I'm sor- You know what? No.
It's time to let go;
And move on from heartache;
You made your mistake,
And I made mine,
Now I just hope you're doing fine.

As you walked out the door;
Across the bleeding floor,
My heart was smashed and strewn;
But I'll be doing better soon.

Echoes

Echoes of beauty dance on the wind;
And scream the loudest when day dawns,
To break the eerie loveless silence;
Black fades to blue and back to black again;
Yet red will never fade away.

Come to terms with what must be;
Yet always mind,
That there is always beauty in the things we cannot see.

It's hard to move on forwards;
When the whole world takes you backwards;
Push against the world and live a life devoted,
To love and life;
Because where am I without it?

To soldier on in solitude through to tinted days?
Or fall behind and wilt;
In the quickly dawning rays?

Eighth World Wonder

Shimmering emerald pools;
A thousand miles deep,
Set upon a gilded angel;
Luminous in darkest times;
To guide the foolish hearts.

Priceless beauty,
Unleashed upon the world;
This jaw aghast at tender lips;
Blushed with the softest rose,
And paper cheeks that never crinkle.

The perfect blank canvas;
For writing loves affection;
Breathe in this beauty;
Here she stands;
The only sight worth seeing.

Yet further still the ink will spill;
For beneath this gilded beauty;
Beats a heart so fair;
If compassion were a game to play,
There'd be no equal anywhere.

With love and kindness coming forth;
This ornate beauty has it all;
A heart so large in size and warmth;
That it transcends the worldly gaze;
To sit her firmly alongside angels;
Never out of place.

Gone Up In Smoke

Charred lips brush across these;
Tonight burned so fast;
But not quite long enough.

The smouldering heart of another,
Douses and cleanses mine;
Black stains on bed sheets burnt;
Caught in the heat of moment;
Melting in the sun;
Lover, you caught me off guard.

You set fire to my heart
And forgot to put it out.

I Am Death

I don't know you;
but I will.
You don't know me;
but you will.

The first time will be the last time.
Suffering is not enough for I am death,
And you will die.

The Void

There is a deepening void within,
I hear the darkness calling;
It beckons in the night like a haunting temptress;
Pulling in the weakest man to kneel before her.

There is no escape from this mighty chasm;
A bottomless pit that steals the breath of life;
Here within these walls there is nothing;
Not a hint of life,
Nor happiness to be found.

Yet after all this is home and I am truly comfortable;
Sinking is easier than fighting;
You won't realise until it's too late,
That this was never the home for you.

Reflection

I never thought the world could find someone as perfect as you, I never thought it was possible. As I stand here knowing this might never be, it breaks what little of a heart I have left. I've given most of it to you, and I want you to take the rest. If I don't have you, I won't need it.

I lay and watch the clouds alone;
Forever chasing the beauty unknown;
My hands ache, muscles weak;
This love was all I ever had to seek.

I can never lose this game;
Nothing would be the same;
I know deep down this is true;
My life is nothing without you.

I never thought perfection could be found;
Yet, my brain, you astound;
My withered heart is breaking;
My tired eyes are aching.

You own my heart;
It's always been yours right from the start;
What's left of it I will not need;
So thank you, my love, my soul you've freed.

Portrait of an Artist

A beautiful portrait tucked away,
Beyond the dusty room;
A great achievement shared no more.

Spared for her own good,
The flame of incandescence was too bright for you;
I could not watch my beauty
Drip,
Drip,
Drip away.

With love I saved your beauty;
Framed forever for all to see;
But now too much time has passed;
And I hope you still remember me.

Thoughts of you have never dwindled;
But I could not watch you melt away;
Above my fireplace you hang my love;
And forever there you'll stay.

Stitched Together

Sunbeams burn new horizons on tepid skies of grey,
Shrouded in mystery beckons the new day;
Heavy air sits light upon the shoulder;
For every sky that burns we feel a little older;
Tomorrow won't be yesterday;
And new skies flame the old away.

A brighter tomorrow comes
And not a moment too soon.

Crescent moon divine,
Resides in glory over humble dwellers,
Searching for meaning in a distant land.

She halts the tide for two beating hearts,
Broken together but placed side by side;
The shivering night holds comfort by moonlight;
Noble lands soak the spilt blood of lovers;
Traipse across the dusty land to mend this splintered heart.

When moonlight comes it's time to run;
And run and run;
From this barren wasteland to abundant soil;
Of blue and green.

For when night comes and she shines so bright;
I know where I want to be tonight.

Hawaiian Dreams

The beauty on the wind;
Rustles hair long thinned;
Dancing on the brain,
Throughout the night and day;
And when I turn around again;
The life I knew has turned away.

Breath in the soul of heaven;
And feel mine slip away.

It could be said beneath my pen;
That I know not where we're going now;
I only hope we find our way.

There's beauty in the sky tonight;
Feel it on your skin.

Elsternwick

How can I explain?
You're there on my tongue from dusk to dawn;
Lurching forward, close to breath;
Endless beauty looks out beyond me.

A desert mirage unattainable;
Too good to believe;
Too good to let go;
Burn bright beyond my mortal eyes;
For you have earned them all.

This face is yours to do with what you will,
Angel skin so soft to touch;
Unable to let go.

Out In the Open

These fated open hearts spin;
Knees weaken, the air gets thin;
Eyes widen and thoughts begin to dance;
Is this my chance?

The boldest eyes that one could see;
The kindest heart known to me;
My mind wanders so effortlessly;
To thoughts of you on dark navy.

In the dark my mind is yours;
Grasping feelings my body ignores;
In my dreams you are again;
It's not a case of if but when.

Our bodies must lie together;
Your golden hair of silk and feather;
Rests upon your shoulder softly;
Fingers entwined oh so fondly.

Those eyes so deep of fragile blue;
Pull me softly back to you;
This is the place I never leave in day or night;
Laying here can only feel so right.

Dead Man Walking

I saw you today;
But never said a word;
Too many things I wanted to say;
That you've already heard.

Is love deaf?
Or is love blind?
Love is death;
I think you'll find.

A Calling

I'm sorry for calling again last night;
I hope the sound of my desperate voice;
Didn't give you too much of a fright;
Feeling this alone was never my choice.

It was never one you wanted to make;
Yet now I'm all alone;
Regurgitating heartache;
And clutching my forgotten phone.

If you never return my call,
At least I'll know this time,
Once and for all;
That you're no longer mine.

Six Words

Bravery is beauty,
And nobody holds a candle to yours.
With a solemn duty,
I fight off demons every night in scores.

In the morning we spoke not much at all,
But only for little bit,
Six words to make the skin crawl,
It's ok, I'm used to it.

How callous the hands that sew pain,
A hideous beast that I despise,
But there shall be no suffering in vain,
Let me wipe the tears from your eyes.

The pain is more acute than ever before,
But I will never quit.
Because those six words haunt me once more;
It's ok, I'm used to it.

Kitchen Tiles

Silent dances warm the coldest feet;
To keep rhythm with your overwhelming beat.
We dance tonight once again;
Like words on paper guided by the pen.

My feet move with yours;
And you feel the way my heart adores,
Every second that we dance without the band,
Twirl and spin, hand in hand.

Changing Seasons

Turn your head toward the sun;
The softest reflection shimmers on the night;
Fragile eyes look deep through me;
How bright your presence can shine;
The sun will be here soon to bring the day.

Gentle hands brush upon the velvet skin of an angel;
Your voice the compass,
Tracing the outline of your perfection with my imperfection;
The night burns on with daybreak in sight;
The sun will be here soon to bring the day.

Within my grasp a lesson for the ages;
There is no substitute for perfection;
As beautiful inside as out;
She changed my life and saves it every day;
The sun will be here soon to bring the day.

Mary Rose

The calmest waters hold steady,
In the face of all who conquer,
This journey for those who are but ready;
And not a moment longer.

From the moment we departed,
Across the ocean blue;
We planned a course well charted,
Yet all the same brand new.

The journey never did run smooth,
When storm clouds descend,
And with nothing left to prove;
The fatal course was penned.

By now we are all to aware,
That the ship did run aground,
Burnt and wrecked beyond repair;
Waiting patiently to be found.

Tatters

I'm falling out of love with love,
And winding down the clock again,
Where once her beauty shone above,
It now lies tattered in a world of pain.

Day 35

My soul is torn apart,
Nothing can soothe this aching heart,
But the thought of every word,
Leaves me longing to be heard.

The way that I loved you,
Could never be anything but true;
Even if we played pretend,
You know I'll love you until the end.

But baby don't say never;
I'll wait for you forever.

Rapunzel

Those silky locks run free,
With careless abandon and lonely glee;
They sway softly in the gentle breeze;
One that lifts the spirits,
And brings about new days with ease.
These days are golden like the sun,
And those threads from which perfect locks are spun.

Delicate flowers too shy to bloom,
For her presence so fair is bright enough,
To light all but a single room.

She means everything to men undeserving,
The jester, the joker, the king.
He loses once more,
This time seems different;
She is no treasure like before.

With a heart of gold,
And eyes so bold;
There is courage there,
I know, I've seen it,
The courageous beauty with the diamond hair.

Let down your hair and pull me in,
Let down your hair and see me grin.

Let down your hair, and save me.
Please.

Emptiness

We never met,
We never will;
And yet,
I'll love you forever still.

June

Nothing excites me anymore;
I grin and bear it for the world;
But nothing is as it was before;
And I dare not show myself unfurled.

I miss the cries I never heard;
The way you'd look up at me,
Hanging on my every word;
A prouder love the world would never see.

It's time to go now I guess;
And as I think of June;
It is clear that I must confess;
My desire to see you soon.

Day 41

Everybody leaves,
Sadly it's a part of life,
Well at least in mine.

The Pursuit of Happiness

I have dedicated my life to you,
I made a promise,
And I will see it through.

I gave you my heart,
It will be only yours,
Together or apart.

This love is forever,
I'll hold out hope,
For better late than never.

Swiss Cheese

Laughing in chaotic tandem,
I forgot myself with careless abandon;
This is my life now,
And if only I could show you how,
That my heart is yours, whatever for,
It's safe with you and I need it no more.

Window

I drowned in her;
Because I could not swim.
She drowned in me;
But was saved by Him.

Broken Pen

The words came easy once,
Now I've learnt that simple pain,
Brings them back again.

If and When

Bare skin flinches under the loneliest breeze,
Empty hands hold nothing but themselves;
And scentless air falls heavy on aching nights like these.

Far away she stirs at night,
Alone with only memories of what once was,
Without the need to reunite.

Tonight's the night I hope to hold her once again,
Speaking truly, that night may never come
But I'll be prepared for if and when.

Ticking Clocks

It's been a year, or has it?
Clocks tick slower by the minute,
And every second creaks into existence;
The dawn of a new day still met with the same resistance.

Dates may change but the time never will,
I'm locked here forever still.

Memories of love burn bright,
I miss you again tonight.

The Long Road to Nowhere

The road.
Oh, the road.
It twists and turns through infuriating chaos,
Yet somehow it never ends.

I'm not sure where I've been,
And I don't know where I'm going.
I'm not sure how I got here,
And I don't know where I am.

Oh, the road.

The road continues on.

About the author

o.b.
thompson

O.B. Thompson is a British poet based in Melbourne, Australia whose emotive and caustic hybrid free verse style combines irregular structures with more traditional language has influences across the spectrum in Hardy, Enright & Duffy.

He is also the founder of Warmbreeze Digital Publishing who are the proud publishers of this work and a number of other wonderful writers.

You can find more from O.B. Thompson at:

obthompson.com
OR
warmbreezepublishing.com

Previous Work

Illustrative (2020)
Stories of my Existential Life (2013, 2021 3rd Edition)
Poetry is Dead (2014, 2021 2nd Edition)
The People's Book

www.ingramcontent.com/pod-product-compliance
Lightning Source LLC
LaVergne TN
LVHW091216080426
835509LV00009B/1028